JOSEPH CONRAD.

NOTES ON JOSEPH CONRAD

WITH SOME
UNPUBLISHED LETTERS,
by ARTHUR SYMONS.

BOOKS FOR LIBRARIES PRESS
FREEPORT, NEW YORK

First Published 1925
Reprinted 1971

INTERNATIONAL STANDARD BOOK NUMBER:
0-8369-5662-1

LIBRARY OF CONGRESS CATALOG CARD NUMBER:
71-148899

PRINTED IN THE UNITED STATES OF AMERICA

FOREWORD.

JOSEPH CONRAD is dead, and there goes with him one of the most original and sinister and sombre personalities of our time, and one of the greatest novelists. When I use the word great, I do not mean to compare him with Balzac, who saw humanity as in a mirror, the humanity which comes to the great dreamers, the great poets, humanity as Shakespeare saw it; and so in Balzac, as in all great artists, there is something more than nature, a divine excess. Yet all the same, Conrad must be coupled with certain giants. He was, to my own personal knowledge, incapable of rest, and incapable of existing without production. Like Whistler, when he was not working at his own art—for which he had the same passionate devotion—he was elaborating a fine art of conversation. "In argument," wrote one of his friends, "he was extremely formidable, with a mellow wisdom, a ripe experience, and an extraordinary capacity for impressing his point of view. He had a fund of scathing contempt for the people or things that aroused his imagination, but his nature was kindly." Conrad created by some inexplicable, by some mysterious, by some occult form of mesmerism, worlds unknown, unimaginable, monstrous and most perilous; and, having created and judged them, I imagine him, squatting like some Satanical spider in his web, in some corner, stealthily hidden away from view, throwing out—almost like *la Pieuvre*—tentacles into the darkness. At the centre of his web sits an elemental sarcasm discussing human affairs with a cynical ferocity; behind that sarcasm crouches some powerful devil, insidious, poisonous, irresistible, spawning evil for his own delight.

Conrad's novels have no plots, and they do not need them ; for, as he said : "invention had that mysterious, almost miraculous power of providing striking effects by means impossible of detection, which is the last word of the highest art." Why is it that no woman has ever been the centre of these stories ? I have asked myself that question in vain : for Conrad is unique in this, that unlike every other great novelist, his women are for the most part nameless shadows. There are wonderful exceptions, such as Aïssa and Nina, who have the fierce charm of the unknown. "We must help them to stay in that beautiful world of their own, lest ours gets worse. Oh, she had to be out of it !" And yet what wonderful understanding of a woman's heart there is in these sentences. "Woman though she was, she could not comprehend, in her simplicity, the tremendous compliment of that speech, that whisper of deadly happiness, so sincere, so spontaneous, coming so straight from the heart—like every corruption. It was the voice of madness, of a delirious peace, of happiness that is infamous, cowardly, and so exquisite that the

8

FOREWORD

debased mind refuses to contemplate its terminations."
Note that significant phrase: "like every corruption." It
means, for one thing, the whole suspense of that falling,
slow, reluctant, irresistible, into the past, that marks the
footsteps of most of his victims on their way to Perdition.

Conrad said to me once—I have never forgotten
it, for, as a matter of fact, I did not believe he really
meant it—"I do not create, I invent." His meaning
probably was, that invention comes before creation.
Take, for instance, Karain, "clothed in the Vision of
unavoidable success," flying before a shadow, comforting
himself with the certainty of a charm. There is Kurtz,
who returns to barbarism, and Tuan Jim with his
sacrifice of life to honour, and even the dying nigger
steersman who, shot through by a spear, looks once
on his master: "and the intimate profundity of that
look which he gave me when he received his hurt
remains to this day in my memory—like a claim of
distant kinship affirmed in a supreme moment." It is
with this agonising clearness, this pitiless mercy, that
Conrad shows us human beings, and he loves them best
because their love is the love of the impossible; he
loves them because they are part of the unknown.

And so it is *Lord Jim* in which his genius has
attained its zenith; with *Karain* and *Heart of Darkness*
close after it. Consider the marvellous art, the suspense,
the evasion of definite statement, the overpowering
profundity of it. To begin with, there is the trick,

9

one of Conrad's inextricable tricks of art, by which suspense is scarcely concerned with action, but with a gradually revealed knowledge of what might have happened in the making of a man. Take an instance in *Nostromo*. There is a Dr. Monyngham who comes in at the beginning of the book, comes and goes briefly up to the 300th page; and then suddenly, apropos of nothing, the whole history of his troubles, the whole explanation of what has seemed mysterious in him, is given in four pages; whereupon the last sentence, four pages back, is caught up and continued with the words : "That is why he hobbled in distress in the Casa Gould on that morning." Now, why is there this kind of hesitation? Why is a disguise kept up so long and thrown off for no apparent reason? It is merely one of his secrets, which is entirely his own; but another of them he has learned from Balzac; the method of doubling or trebling the interest by setting action within action, as a picture is set within a frame.

In *Lord Jim* Conrad has revealed more finally than elsewhere, his ideal; the ideal of an applauded heroism, the necessity of adding to one's own conviction the world's acceptance and acclamation. "Man is amazing, but he is not a masterpiece," says someone in the book, one of the many types and illustrations of men who have fallen into a dream, all with some original sin to proclaim or conceal or justify, one crowding on another. Amazing they may be, but Jim, "approaching greatness as genuine as any man ever achieved," with the shame of his "jump" from a sinking ship and his last fearless jump "into the unknown," his last "extraordinary success," when, in one proud and unflinching glance, he beholds "the face of that opportunity which, like an Eastern bride, had come veiled to his side"; amazing he may be, but a masterpiece, proved, authentic, justifying Man.

To read Conrad is to shudder on the edge of a gulf, in a silent darkness. *Karain* is full of mystery, *Heart of Darkness* of an unholy magic. "The fascination of the abomination—you know," the teller of the story says for him, and "Droll thing life is." The whole narrative is an evocation of that "stillness of an implacable brooding over an incalculable intention."

There can be no question of the fact that Conrad's genius is abnormal He invented a manner of writing which was wholly his own, and a manner so original that it baffles all possible conjectures as to how he created it; and with this the lacerating laughter of Rabelais; and, besides this, an almost Japanese art of spiritual dislocation; and, when he wanted to take his revenge upon science, borrowing its very terms, making them dance at the end of a string, derisively; and, like Lafargue, thinking intensely about life, he seized on what is automatic, pathetically ludicrous in it, almost as one might who has no part in the comedy; who is one with Villiers only in this: that it was part of his curiosity in souls to prefer the complex to the simple, the perverse to the

b   11 straightforward, the ambiguous to either. And this casuist of souls, Villiers, will drag forth some horribly stunted or horribly overgrown soul from under its obscure covering, setting it to dance naked before our eyes. So did Conrad.

Conrad, I think, had no pity on himself or on anything that annoyed him; and yet he was the proudest man I have ever met and could be one of the most lovable. Inscrutable, at times as impenetrable as one of his dense and formidable, menacing and monstrous jungles, there was something in his aspect which struck me as being almost inhuman: not the absolute inhumanity of Pachmann —who is as inhuman as the music he plays—but inhuman in much the same sense, because he also showed a physical disquietude which was but a sign of what it cost him to venture outside humanity. There is almost as much fever in Conrad's most exasperated prose as when, feverishly, you see Pachmann's fingers feeling after the sound of the notes, his face calling to them, his whole body imploring them. Therefore, Conrad's prose has in it something fantastically inhuman, like fiery ice, and it is for this reason that it remains a thing uncapturable, a thing whose secret he himself could never reveal; and with this an almost incalculable fascination, as of some bizarre masquerade in which the devil plays pranks, and has thus at least an immovable centre to whirl from. When a soul plays dice with the devil there is only a second in which to win or lose: but the second may be worth an Eternity.

I NEVER knew to what extent Joseph Conrad was fascinating. When I first set eyes on him, in 1911, I was fairly startled : there stood before me a Dwarf of Genius ; and what further startled me was that he was about the same height as Toulouse Lautre, whom I had known in Paris—he was a much more formidable Dwarf of Genius, who died tragically young. Conrad expired suddenly, at the age of sixty-seven, in full possession of his powers, and, as he fell dead on the floor from the chair he was seated on, I am told he uttered a great cry. So, as I was assured, did Rossetti, who rose up in his bed and cried out violently, as if he had seen before him the Vision of Hell. Conrad, essentially himself, always, even when he was most exasperated, most malicious, most bewildering, most enchanting, flamed before one as a man of genius, if ever there was one ; unique, in his own way, abnormal, not wholly normal, I noticed how the muscles of the face, as well as the wrinkles, were visibly at work, and how sudden, convulsive and indicative were his gestures. Pater, in *Gaston de Latour*, represents Ronsard as " A gaunt figure, hook-nosed, like a wizard, who turned you a face all nerves, distressed nerves, and not un-kindly." That gives a certain idea of Conrad's aspect. He was exotically cruel; there was a tropical heat in his blood; he vibrated to every sensation, as Verlaine vibrated, as Pachmann vibrates; and, as in the case of Pachmann, there was his indisputable foreign accent, which began by surprising one, but which was really part of his fascination—for he had a fascinating fashion of talking, always, whether in English or French, with great rapidity and with a wonderful power of evocation which, when it thrilled him most, thrilled me. He had at times the same convulsive chuckle as Verlaine's; his laughter when he was most excited reminded me of Whistler's sharp crackle of laughter, which was as if a rattlesnake had suddenly leapt out; which was in fact a crackling of thorns under the pot, but of flaming thorns, setting the pot in a fury of boiling.

Marlow, being in a sense Conrad's familiar ghost, evokes in this vision of Lord Jim—it might be one of Conrad's less familiar ghosts—a vision of his creator. "The muscles round his lips contracted into an un-conscious grimace that tore through the mask of his usual expression—something violent, short-lived and illuminating, like a flash of lightning that admits the eye for an instant into the secret convolutions of a cloud." Conrad's burning and penetrating dark brown eyes, which changed and shifted as his nerves and his moods shifted and changed, were as variable as opals,

14

and under his black brows they had that terrible fixity of vision which, like a cat's, is inexorable; eyes, that having in their deep sorcerous depths something of the sea's glamour, had never forgotten the sea.

This is one of his confessions. " May there not emerge at last the vision of a personality; the man behind the books so fundamentally dissimilar as for instance, *Almayer's Folly* and *The Secret Agent*—and yet a coherent justifiable personality both in its origin and in its actions ? " In 1907 he wrote to me, thanking me for my " rejected address to the public on behalf of his art, and for the warm, living sincerity of my impression and of my analysis." He confesses that " fourteen years of honest work are not gone for nothing. A big slice of life that, which I may say is not altogether lost. There has been in all the time not ten minutes of amateurishness. That is the truth. For the rest I may say that there are certain passages in your article which have surprised me. I did not know that I had ' a heart of darkness ' and ' an unlawful soul.' Mr. Kurtz had—and I have not treated him with easy nonchalance. Believe me, no man ever paid more for his lines than I have. But then I possess an inalienable right to the use of all my epithets. The fact is that I am really a much simpler person. Death is a fact—and violent death is a fact too. In the simplicity of my heart I tried to realise these facts when they came in. Do you really think that Flaubert gloated over the death bed of Emma, or the death march of Mâtho, or the last moments of Felicie? I've never looked into myself. There was no time in these years to turn my head away from the table. There are whole days when I did not know whether the sun shone or not. And, after all, the books are there! As for the writing of novels, delightful or not, I have always approached my task in the spirit of love for mankind. And I've rather taken it seriously. But I stand outside and feel grateful to you for the recognition of the work—not the man. Once the last page is written the man does not count. He is nowhere."

In that confession Conrad is one with Flaubert, in love with art, in love with life, in love with creation, and in the final self-effacement of the artist. It is interesting to note that he had finished reading *Salammbo* before he began *The Nigger of the Narcissus* and that the sailors in the forecastle of the ship are filled in with a similar touch to the barbarians in the garden of Hamilcar.

Conrad certainly accepted as a matter of pure faith these sayings of Flaubert. " The determination to give to prose the rhythm of verse, leaving it still veritable prose ; to write the story of common life as history or the epic gets written (that is to say, without detriment to the natural truth of the subject) is perhaps impossible. I ask myself this question sometimes. Yet it is perhaps a conceivable, an original thing, to have tried. I shall have had my permanent value for my obstinacy. And who knows? One day I may find a good *motif*, an air entirely within the compass of my voice; and at any rate I shall have passed my life not ignobly, often with delight." The next letter I had from Conrad is written in exactly the same spirit of devotion and of a kind of consecration and indeed a passion for one's art as Flaubert's.

"One thing that I am certain of, is that I have approached the object of my task, things human, in a spirit of piety. The earth is a temple where there is going on a mystery play childish and poignant, ridiculous and awful enough in all conscience. Once in I've tried to behave decently. I have not degraded the quasi religious sentiment by tears and groans : and if I have been amused and indifferent, I've neither grinned nor gnashed my teeth. In other words I've tried to write with dignity, not only out of regard of myself, but for the sake of the spectacle, the play with an obscure beginning and an unfathomable *denouement*. I don't think this has been noticed. It is your penitent beating the floor with his forehead and the ecstatic worshippers at the rails that are obvious to the public eye. The man standing quietly in the shadow of the pillar if noticed at all runs the risk of being suspected of sinister designs. As I wrote to a friend I have been quarrying my English out of a black night, working like a coal miner in his pit. For fourteen years now

I have been living as if in a cave without echoes. If you come shouting gloriously at the mouth of the same you can't really expect me to pretend I am not there."

Conrad wrote : " I know that a novelist lives in his work. He stands there, the only reality in an invented world, amongst imaginary things, happenings and people. Writing about them, he is only writing about himself. Every novel contains an element of autobiography—and this can hardly be denied, since the creator can only explain himself in his creations." So did Balzac, who would find out God, as he comes nearer and nearer to finding out the secret of life ; and would pursue the soul to its last resting-place before it takes flight from the body ; in whom—in whom alone—a devouring passion of thought burned on all the situations by which humanity expresses itself, in its flight from the horror of immobility. Stendhal does not, Zola does not, Goncourt does not, Maupassant does not. These, to my mind at least, are outside and not inside their invented world—they never write about themselves. Flaubert, Rabelais, Cervantes, Meredith, Hardy, Emily Brontë, are inside and not outside of their invented world. In the passionately tragic genius of Emily Brontë I find a primitive nature-worship. The spirit inexorable to the flesh ; there is the whole secret of what in her life was her genius ; at times there is a tragical sublimity in her imagination, which gathers together, as it were, the winds from the world's four quarters ; and in *Wuthering Heights* there are startling scenes and sentences which once impressed on the memory, are unforgettable ; as scarlet flowers of evil and as poisonous weeds they take root in one. I do not know any novelist who, before Meredith and Conrad, has brought into fiction so much of the atmosphere of poetry, with so much of the actual art of composition of the poet, as Hawthorne ; who, seeing always " a grim identity between gay things and sorrowful ones " sets a masquerade before us, telling us many of the secrets hidden behind the black velvet, but letting us see no more than the glimmer of eyes, and the silent or ambiguous lips.

How is it that few novelists except Conrad—my exceptions are Rabelais, Balzac, Flaubert, Tolstoi, Hawthorne and Emily Brontë—have got to that hidden depth, where the soul really lives and dies, where, in an almost perpetual concealment, it works out its plan, its own fate ? Even he himself could not have explained it. With San Juan de la Cruz the obscure night is a way, the negation of all earthly things, of one's senses even, a means to the final union with God ; pierce the dark night to its centre, and you will find light, for you will find God. Hawthorne is haunted by what is obscure, dangerous, and on the confines of good and evil ; by what is abnormal, indeed (as in the case of Conrad) if we are to accept human nature as a thing set within responsible limits ; only, unlike Conrad, who does not apprehend Sin in the manner of the Mystics, but as a thing to be carefully avoided, which inevitably brings its own punishment upon itself, finding the soul, in its essence, so intangible, so mistlike, that he lays hold of what to him is the only great reality, Sin, in order that he may find out something definite about the soul. " Not supernatural, but just on the verge of nature, and yet within it ; " that is where he sets himself to surprise the soul's last secrets ; he responds to every sensation of the soul, morbidly ; he is at home in all those cloudy tracts of the soul's regions in which most novelists go astray.

" A man who never wrote a line for print before he was thirty-six cannot bring himself to look back upon his existence and his experiences, upon the sum of his thoughts, sensations and emotions, upon his memories and regrets, and the whole possession of his past, as only so much material for his hands. I wanted to pay my tribute to the sea, its ships and its men, to whom I remain so much indebted for so much which has gone to make me what I am." It is by his vision and his imagination and his creation that Conrad will live. The vision of the sea, a vision which might prove to be more faithful than even a passionate lover's faith to his mistress—if indeed that were possible, and, as we know, such possibilities exist and might for all one conjectures exist for ever—a vision which

JOSEPH CONRAD

embraces not only the sea's limits but the sea's infinities, which are like hell's most dire infinities, and those invincible waves which when tempest tossed cause more restlessness on the sea's surface together with the intolerable heaving of the whole sea's fury around a shattered ship than the sustained booming of the wind and the distant roaring of the ocean before its final upheaval. There have been many writers about the sea, but only Conrad has loved it with so profound and yet untrustful a love. His storms have sublimity, made out of intense attention to detail, heightened into tragedy by the shifting floor and changing background on which is represented the vast struggle of man with the powers of nature. And as he loves the earth only in its extravagances, so he loves the sea most in storms, where love and fear mingle.

Conrad said to me : " Fenimore Cooper is a rare artist. He has been one of my masters. He is my constant companion." This he enlarged in a notice of Cooper and of Marryat. " To this writer of the sea, Marryat, the sea was not an element. To the multitude of readers the navy of to-day is Marryat's navy still. He perhaps loved not the sea at all. But the sea loved him without reserve." On the contrary Cooper loved the sea and looked at it with a consummate understanding. " Through the distance of time and space these two men of another race have shaped the life of the writer of this appreciation. In testimony to the achievement of these authors, it may be said that, in the case of the writer at least, the youthful glamour, the headlong vitality of the one, and the profound sympathy, the artistic insight of the other—to which he had surrendered—have withstood the brutal shock of facts and the wear of laborious years. He has never regretted his surrender."

In Conrad's prose one finds a peculiar flavour, fiery and fervent, when he chooses to fuse imaginative passion with sarcastic realism. Here and there this strange Polish temperament—which is essentially unlike that of the Russians, a temperament which has its roots in Pessimism and in emotion, in the sincerity of the savage, in the practical logic which sets men and women outside the laws, for good or evil, deliberately —has expressed itself in a few words, a significant silence ; and what we have felt is just what is deepest and most profound, most mysterious and most menacing, most sombre and most sullen, in that nature of his, which listens to a voice which is not of the blood, which listens to a voice which is the vital and vehement voice of the blood.

II.

ABNORMALITY is the keynote of Conrad's creative genius. I choose by way of example the first sentence of *An Outcast of the Islands*. " When he stepped off the straight and narrow path of his peculiar honesty, it was with an inward assertion of conflicting resolve to fall back again into the monotonous but safe stride of virtue as soon as his little excursion into the wayside quagmires had produced the desired effect." That is abnormal, but not quite " a sentence in brackets, so to speak." " The incorruptible Professor walked too, averting his eyes from the odious multitude of mankind. He walked frail, insignificant, shabby, miserable —and terrible in the simplicity of his idea calling madness and despair to the regeneration of the world. Nobody looked at him. He passed on unsuspected and deadly, like a pest in the street full of men." That is the abnormal end of *The Secret Agent*, a book itself as deadly and as poisonous as some ravaging pestilence ; Beddoes might have made something, within a brief space, of this nightmare subject ; the subject being that a certain " particular fiend " drives Verloc into a cruel blunder and his wife into a madness, a murder, a suicide, which combine into one chain, link after link, inevitably.

Now, in a certain sense, Poe, who was fantastically inhuman, a conscious artist doing strange things with strange materials, whose genius was flawed by something meretricious in it, could be at times, but rarely, almost as infallible as Baudelaire. " A skilful literary artist has constructed a tale. If wise, he has not fashioned his thoughts to accommodate his incidents ; but having conceived, with deliberate care, a certain unique or single effect to be wrought out, he then invents such incidents—he then combines such events as may best aid him in establishing this preconceived effect. If his initial sentences tend not to the out-bringing of this effect, then he has failed in his first step. In the whole composition there should be no word written, of which the tendency, direct or indirect, is not to the one pre-established design." That, to a certain extent, is infallible ; but, as a matter of fact, he demands the impossible. As there are rules to every exception, Poe certainly in a dozen or more of his wonderful, abnormal, terrible and overwhelming stories has achieved the impossible. I need only mention *The Pit and the Pendulum* and *The Cask of Amontillado*. I would say the same of a dozen of the monstrous and marvellous, the unsurpassable and atrocious, the bizarre and ironical, cruel and complex, stories of Villiers de l'Isle-Adam. But I could not say this of any of Conrad's, in which there is neither plot nor counter-plot. And yet, when one thinks of it,

JOSEPH CONRAD

how much there is, in his genius, of the dramatic and the tragic; and as in the case of Tourneur, of whom Swinburne wrote : " There is no such relief to the terrors of the maturer work, whose sultrier darkness is visible only by the fire kindled of itself, very dreadful, which burns in the heart of the revenger whom it lights along his bloodstained way."

The morbid sense of life, everywhere impressed on the very atmosphere of that sombre story, *Madame Bovary,* came certainly from the writer himself. " The cruelty of the way of things," wrote Pater, " that is a conviction of which the development is partly traceable in his letters." The cruelty of human nature—what is it ? And how is it that it has struck so deep ? Because it has an individual, abominable attraction, a fascination, for almost everyone ; for many of us, under scrupulous disguises : but the principle is there, deeply rooted in nature. *An Outpost of Progress* contains horrors unspeakable ; it is conceived as Swift might have conceived an almost insane satire, it is brought to birth by some primeval sarcasm ; where two existences, Carlier's and Kayert's, aimless and impotent, clash and clatter like two broken earthenware pots. One might call it a charnel-house curiosity ; the fascination of corruption as in the case of Baudelaire, who was more amorous of corruption than Beddoes ; or of Poe, who was more spellbound by the scent of graveyard earth. And, indeed, in this one story at

NOTES ON

by Arthur Sy

least, Conrad has become the chronicler of the praise
and ridicule of Death.

Among the fundamental traits of his genius are
the sense of suspense, of madness, of craft, of some
unutterable thirst, of the unknown—with all its allure-
ments and attractions and repulsions—and most of all,
and most wonderfully and fearfully conveyed, is the
sense of fear, fear inevitable, unavoidable, unfathomable,
inexplicable ; a thing as mysterious as the night which
hides all things, and as death which, blindly, hides all
things. Verloc comes to his end because he must get
a visible fear out of his eyes ; Alvan abandons his wife
because he cannot get the hated sight of her out of his
eyes ; there is James Wait, the nigger, the dying man,
supported in his horrible fear of death by the shadowy
and sinister splendour of his own presence : " The
tragic, the mysterious, the repulsive mask of a nigger's
soul." Think of Sotillo. " Every time he went in
and came out with a slam of the door, the sentry on
the landing presented arms, and got in return a black,
venomous, unsteady glance, which, in reality, saw
nothing at all, being merely the reflection of the soul
within—a soul of gloomy hatred, irresolution, avarice
and fury." No novelist, not even Balzac, could have
summed up the shocking blackness of a man's heart—
giving, in fact, like a flash of lightning, the entire
mask—as Conrad does in this sentence. And yet, to
return to my starting point, is not that sentence itself

abnormal ? In such sentences as these relative values are lost, and the world, in this strange disorder of vision, assumes an aspect which can only be compared with that of a drop of impure water under the microscope.

A critic said : " Conrad's characters are subject to *idees fixes* springing from contact with an essentially mad world," which, as a statement, can hardly be denied ; it cannot be denied in the characters of Dostoievsky, who probed to the depths of men's insane souls and men's and women's diseased bodies with an amazing fixity of purpose, and with a genius certainly degenerate. " Blake," wrote Richard Curle, " is an extraordinarily dynamic artist and Dostoievsky the greatest novelist the world is ever likely to see, but I am quite sure that neither of them is sane in the sense that Conrad is sane—as sure as that their " insanity " is so subtle and indefinable that I will never be able to lay my finger on it." No wonder—for no one could ever dare to lay his finger on Blake—or to point it rather—and to say that Blake was mad. It is true that Blake was abnormal ; but what was abnormal in him was his sanity. To one who believed that " The ruins of time build mansions in Eternity," that " Imagination is Eternity," there could be none of that confusion at the edge of mystery which makes a man mad because he is unconscious of the gulf. Most of his art is the unclothing of the soul, and when at last it is naked and alone, in that thrilling region where the souls of other men have at times penetrated, only to shudder back with terror from the brink of eternal loneliness, then only is the soul exultant with the supreme happiness. Conrad shudders back from that brink, not from the edge of mystery, not daring to let the soul he has created fly naked.

Only great painters have created atmosphere to the extent that Conrad has; and Conrad's is if anything more mysterious, menacing, and more troubling to the senses and to the nerves, than theirs; he creates thrilling effects by mere force of suggestion, elusive as some vague mist, full of illusion, of rare magic, which can become poisonous and sorcerous. " The mysterious East faced me, perfumed like a flower, silent like death, dark like a grave." And in the very midst and in the heart or all this his figures, for all their enormous variety, fix themselves upon one's imagination. It is not from character merely, or merely a choice from among emotions, as one emotion comes interestingly into a face, or the gesture which renders the outward man so that we may recognise him in the street; it is a brooding unconsciousness, coming up into the eyes and fixed there in all its restlessness; the inner mystery itself, not the explaining away of that mystery; the ultimate dumbness of the soul, as trivial things drop away from it, and it stands lonely, questioning, unfathomably secret. For every soul—

JOSEPH CONRAD

Shakespeare knew this as absolutely and without the least terror at the bare thought of it or of its strange sensations as Balzac and Rodin—has its own way of being silent, of looking into the darkness at the end of the long avenue, of knowing how little it can ever know, and how much of wisdom lies in that acquiescence.

The agony of creation must be, I imagine, to most artists, not unlike the travail of a child in a mother's womb. Conrad creates great crises, tragic and inevitable, ironical and vital and violent; and these crises, which occur as the mainspring of most of his narratives, almost always end in some tremendous climax which at once arrests and rivets one's attention—and so intensely that one seems to swirl with them in the disastrous turmoil of their lusts and greeds and passions, and rarely with any sense of relief from the poignancy of these situations. Then comes the sting, certain and sudden; and, then, the revulsion.

It seems to me that Conrad has said almost the final, it might be the fundamental, word on Proust— which in certain senses might be applied to himself. " The important thing is that whereas before we had analysis allied to creative art, great in poetic conception, in observation, or in style, his is a creative art absolutely based on analysis. He is a writer who has pushed analysis to the point when it becomes creative. Françoise, the devoted servant, and the Baron de

Charlug, a consummate portrait—how many descriptive lines have they got to themselves in the whole body of that immense work? In that prose so full of life there is no reverie, no emotion, no marked irony, no warmth of sunshine, not even a marked rhythm to charm our ear. What amazes one is its inexplicable character."

What amazes me is what is inexplicable in Conrad, who has many gifts that Proust never had—all those for instance he enumerated—and besides these a creative genius which was not based on analysis, a wonderful power of evocation, an almost unflagging invention which, though one of the lesser forms of creation, is to me almost without parallel in literature. Balzac's of course, was at once unflagging and sleepless. Conrad, however, created a style which in its way is unique, and a rhythm of his own which is, if any rhythm ever was in English, unique.

It was after a severe and prolonged illness that I received this letter from Conrad, in the year 1910. " I have just finished reading your touching and sympathetic letter. No, my dear fellow. You have not deserved it; and if anyone has the right to ask: Why? you have that right. But if you do such things as your translation of *Crimen Amoris* out of despair— then, take my word for it, you need not despair. One survives everything—disaster, annihilation itself, absurd as it seems to say it. Your *desir de vivre* is the best

JOSEPH CONRAD

proof that you deserve to live. And you must not forget that you *exist pour les esprits d'elite* which is the best sort of existence. To recommend forgetfulness to a man so profoundly tried as you have been tried, would be folly. Yet, as has been said, life is a dream, or, as I should say, a succession of songes doux ou terribles. Well, and if it is so, then even in terror we may find inspiration once we regain courage enough to turn our eyes always from it. Don't look back, for indeed the only way to overcome injustice whether of men or fate is to disregard it. Yours,

J. CONRAD."

No one can imagine the encouragement that letter gave me—for never was I more in need of such an encouragement—coming as it did, and with such warmth and such conviction of soul, from a man whose genius I had admired immensely. I turned to a drawer in my desk and drew out a bundle of letters from Eleonora Duse, the greatest actress in the world and the most wonderful woman I had ever known, a woman of supreme genius, and I read this sentence : *Je vous souhaite force et confiance de vivre.*

Conrad said to me once, in a tone of tragic and almost passionate pathos I shall never forget : " Could you conceive for a moment that I could go on existing if Cunninghame Graham were to die ? " Graham, as Conrad always did, expresses himself in a personal way ; is always like some vivid friend talking at one's

side. In his haste to catch that difficult note of
the voice, to appear to be improvising, he sometimes forgets to begin a sentence, or forgets that
he has begun it. But, at his best, he has a
quality of bringing remote scenes before one, with
all the heat of an adventure actually happening, and
with a more exciting interest than perhaps any writer
of the day, with the one exception of Conrad, of whom
his writings sometimes reminds me. Conrad is a
creative artist, while Graham is a chronicler of personal
adventure; but there is something in both of that
splendid subtle recklessness in writing English, which
is a singularly exhilarating quality when used as both
use it, in the record of life lived rapidly, unthinkingly,
in the presence of danger. It is from such writers
that we learn, among other useful lessons, that life
may be more than books, but that books made cun-
ningly out of life can recapture almost the whole of
its escaping present—and certainly less than we know
of the soul and the nerves of a man. A dreamer with
a passion for action, one whose dreams are action, yet
whose actions are certainly for the most part dreams,
Cunninghame Graham brings a touch of the Elizabethan
spirit into contemporary life, urgent, unpractical,
haughty, at war with the world, yet loving the world
for its own sake. He has all the sympathy of what
is really indifferent, and he goes his way interested by
everyone, stopping for no one, a wanderer with so

JOSEPH CONRAD

many purposes as to be without a purpose, Don Quixote with something of the humorous soul of Sancho Panza.

III.

I HAVE said Conrad's novels have no plot, do not even need them; that they are a series of studies in temperaments, deducted from slight incidents; studies in emotion, with hardly a rag to hold together the one or two scraps of action, out of which they are woven. No novel ever made a thing so vital as *Lord Jim*, where there is no plot. In *En Route* of Huysmans one finds the revelation of the sub-conscious self, no longer the intelligence but the soul. This confession is a kind of thinking aloud. It fixes, in precise words, all the uncertainties, the contradictions, the unreasonableness and not less absurd logic, which distract man's brain in the passing over him of sensation and circumstance. And all this thinking is concentrated on one end, is concerned with the working out, in his own singular way, of one man's salvation. Now, is not *Lord Jim*, essentially, this slow, insidious, uncertain, and yet finally certain, working out of that one man's salvation? From birth to death one might imagine his existence as a kind of Penitent's Pilgrimage, which begins when by sheer instinct he jumps off the sinking ship, and which ends gloriously when he gives up his life for a dead man's sake, sending left and right at all the faces of that heaving crowd of armed Bugis a proud

and unflinching glance. " It is when we try to grapple
with another man's need," wrote Conrad, " that we
perceive how incomprehensible, wavering, and misty
are the beings that share with us the sight of the stars
and the warmth of the sun." The force of mere
curiosity can go far, can penetrate to a certain depth ;
yet there is a point at which mere curiosity, even that
of genius, comes to an end ; and we are left to the
individual soul's apprehension of what seems to it the
reality of spiritual things. Such a personal apprehension comes to us out of this book, and at the same
time, just as in the days when Conrad forced language
to express in a more coloured way than it ever had
before, the last escaping details of material things, so,
in this analysis of the warfares and aberrations, the
trials and confessions of the soul in penitence, he
has found words for even the most illusive and subtle
aspects of that inner life which is the soul's.

The prose play, the novel, which came into being as
exceptions, are invented by men who cannot write plays
in verse, cannot write epics ; and, the usurper once
firmly settled, a new dynasty begins, which we come
to call legitimate, as is the world's way with all
dynasties. The novel and the prose play are the two
great imaginative forms which prose has invented for
itself. Prose is the language of what we call real life,
and it is only in prose that an illusion of external
reality can be given. Compare, not only the sur-

roundings, the sense of time, locality, but the whole process and existence of character, in a play of Shakespeare and a novel of Balzac. I choose Balzac among novelists, because his mind is nearer to what is creative in the poet's mind than that of any novelist, and his method nearer to the method of the poet. Take King Lear and take Père Goriot. Goriot is a Lear at heart, and he suffers the same tortures and humiliations. Goriot grows downward into the earth and takes root there, wrapping the dust about all his fibres. Thus, when Balzac triumphs, he triumphs signally; and action, in his books, is perpetually crystallizing into some phrase, like the single lines of Dante, or some brief scene, in which a whole entanglement comes sharply and suddenly to a luminous point.

This is certainly not the method of Conrad. He is much more like Tolstoi than Balzac in his methods ; for one thing, in a very stealthy method of surprising life, life being always the cunning enemy one must lull asleep or noose by an unexpected lasso. A novelist with style will not look at life with an entirely naked vision. Conrad, who created his style with immense difficulty, looks at life with an almost naked vision. Merimée's vision is that of the curious student, the man of the world, ironical, refined, cynical, indifferent. Was there not in him a certain drying up of the sources of emotion, as the man of the world comes to accept almost the view of society, reading his stories

JOSEPH CONRAD

to a little circle of Court ladies, when, once in a while, he permitted himself to write a story? Permitted himself! What a curious lack of inspiration that phrase indicates! Yes, and it is Pater who says the right thing: " It is as if, in theological language, he were incapable of grace." Indeed, if we were to accept the phrase, ' theological language,' what creative novelist could ever be capable of grace?

The rarest subtlety in prose is its physiological quality; for prose listens at the doors of all the senses, and repeats their speech almost in their own tones. There is no form of art which is not an attempt to capture life, but to create life over again. But art, in verse, being strictly and supremely an art, begins by transforming. Prose fiction transforms, it cannot help transforming; but by its nature it is able to follow line for line in a way that verse can never do. The psychological narrative, from which the modern novel of analysis may be said to have arisen, is simply a human document. To the mystic who was Blake, and to the artist who was Conrad the whole world is mysterious. There are the experts who tell one that this world, and life, and the flowing of times past into times to come, are but a simple matter after all; the jarring of this atom against that, a growth by explicable degrees from a germ perhaps not altogether inexplicable. Not of such is the true lover, the true poet. To him woman is as mysterious as the night of stars, and all he learns

JOSEPH CONRAD

of her is but to deepen the mystery which surrounds
her as with clouds.   To him she is fate, an unconscious
part of what is eternal in things, an illumining and a
devouring flame, the Mystical Rose, the female half of
that harmony of opposites which is God.

ARTHUR SYMONS.

MA